Introduction

Formerly, oats were the only grain crop grown in regions of high altitude where the climate was damp and the soil poor — in parts of Scotland, Wales, Staffordshire, Westmorland, Lancashire and Yorkshire. There, oatmeal used for porridge, hasty pudding, and above all for oatcake, formed the basis of the diet. In the Pennine Dales of the West and North Ridings of Yorkshire, which concern us here, two distinct types of oatcake were made: a thin, long, oval-shaped thrown oatcake in the West Riding valleys; and a rolled-out, thicker round cake in the North Riding dales, that is Wensleydale and Swaledale. Both were baked on backstones, but of totally different sorts.

References to oatcake occur in the fourteenth century, and continue over the centuries. They reveal the different kinds of cake baked in the different regions of Yorkshire and the different names, such as havercake (from the Norse *halfri* meaning oats), riddlecake, clapcake, and most telling of all, oatbread, riddlebread and clapbread. In 1674 Ray in *North Country Words* gives clapbread, riddlebread and riddlecake. In 1698 Celia Fiennes reached Kendal on her journeys, and recorded clapbread being made at Kendal by beating by hand a thick paste on a concave board. In 1760 it was being made in Dentdale 'i Keeaks as thick as my finger, and *stoult* in a frying pan'.

The place-name Bakestone Gill, where presumably stone was quarried for making backstones, occurs in several dales, for instance in

Nidderdale and Wensleydale. 'Backstone' remained the term for the implement on which oatcake was baked, whether of stone, mudstone or iron, large or small. The Bakestone Quarry at Delph, near Oldham, formerly in the West Riding, once supplied small, flat mudstone bakestones, hawked on horseback in the industrial West Riding. By 1814 large bakestones, built in kitchen or out-house, had been introduced *(see pages 1, 32-35)*. These were cast-iron plates, set in a structure with a firebox, adjacent to the fireplace or in an outhouse. Bakestones proliferated in farmhouses in the rural West Riding dales. Large bakestones for commercial bakers, invented by Joseph Wright, ironfounder of Shipley, in the middle of the last century, were installed in bakeries in the West Riding. Bakers supplied the influx of workers drawn to live there to find work. There were said to be fifty such bakeries in Bradford.

The home baking of oatcake required skill, and *Gleanings in Craven* by F Montagu (1838) gives a detailed description of making the West Riding type of oatcake. The meal was mixed overnight in a kneading tub, which was scraped out with a knife, leaving particles which fermented to act as a rising agent for the next baking. The bakestone is heated by a fire in the firebox using wood, ling, coal, furze or anything to hand. Meal is sprinkled on the backboard *(see page 14)*, and a ladleful of batter poured on to it. The backboard is reeled (rotated), the batter transferred to a piece of linen or harden on a spittle. Then it is thrown on to the bakestone with a strong jerk, and the linen taken up. After baking for a minute, the cake is turned and baked for another minute, then placed on the *fleeak*, or flake, to dry. The flake consisted of a framework hung from the kitchen beams, and strung with string or wooden lats on which the limp oatcake is hung. The Rev Alfred Easther in his *Glossary of the Dialect of Almondbury and Huddersfield* (1883) described the same process and calls the kneading tub a *nakit*.

This laborious and skilful process of oatcake baking in the home was modified around the middle of the last century by the introduction of a scraper. A pool of batter was poured directly on to the bakestone, and the scraper, which had two nails on the bottom, was drawn across this, the nails giving the required width, and making the thin oval shape. As before it was hung to dry on the flake.

In the case of commercial bakeries using a large bakestone, the throwing action was achieved by a small bogy on wheels, covered with mole cloth and fixed at one end of the bakestone, sometimes called a tram. A pool of batter was placed on the cloth, and, by cranking the tram with a lever and propelling it forward, the batter was thrown on to the hotplate of the bakestone to make a thin oval cake. This could be eaten soft immediately, or hung to dry when it became hard. Easther wrote of the industrial West Riding that 'Oatcake is seldom made by any but public bakers'.

In the North Riding dales of Wensleydale and Swaledale, the baking of oatcake, here called 'havercake', followed an entirely different procedure, more allied to Scottish methods. A thick mixture of oatmeal, salt and water was rolled out with a rolling pin into a circular shape, placed on a portable round bakestone with a handle to hang over the fire, baked, turned, and finished off on the cake stool or cake-dog *(pages 44 and 45)*.

In the mid-1960s and early 70s, when we toured the Dales and the industrial West Riding in search of oatcake, we found that baking in the farmhouse had gone, but that methods, recipes and baking days were still fresh in people's minds. They looked back to memories of large families and hired servants, for whom oatcake was economical food.

In Ribblesdale we heard that two kinds were made: riddlebread, baked on a bakestone; and clapbread, in which the batter was clapped out by hand. We even heard of someone who had baked as described by Montagu using a piece of brown paper on the spittle. Some baked once a month, others made quantities ready for lambing, hay, and salving times. Some used buttermilk after butter-making instead of water, some added carbonate of soda, a few a knob of fat, and a few used yeast. In Malhamdale a tub of batter left overnight was marked with a cross to ward off witches. Havercakes, riddlecakes or riddlebread were stored in a havercake scuttle, basket or in a drawer, or wrapped in a white cloth on shelves hung from the ceiling. It was eaten regularly for breakfast and supper, and broken into broth.

Oatmeal was kept in a meal ark (chest) or in pottery jars. When well pressed down, it kept a long time. We heard of two farms where the farm man, wearing white socks, trampled it down in the ark.

In the industrial West Riding there were two bakers at Skipton in the late 1950s. The Leaches bakehouse had been established in 1858. In their time, as its production faded out, oatcake was sold to Fortnum and Mason, Chatsworth House and so on, and became gourmet fare.

We ourselves were able to photograph Mr and Mrs Leslie Feather in their bakehouse at Haworth. Leslie Feather retired in 1975.

But oatcake is still made at Stanleys Crumpets at Barnoldswick near Skipton. (Barnoldswick was formerly in Yorkshire, and after boundary changes is now in east Lancashire.) Mrs Betty Wordsworth, the owner and oatcake baker at Stanleys, has given us the following details. The large cast-iron bakestone/hotplate is heated by gas jets, and can accommodate three rows of four oatcakes. The tram or trolley holds four pools of oatcake batter, but only two are made at once. First a short jerk of the trolley, and then a good sharp jerk sends the batter on to the hotplate to form the thin elongated shape. After a minute, these are turned and moved to a cooler part of the plate. Thus oatcake, made in the old style, thrown on a bakestone, and sold to customers far and wide, is still made.

Photographic Acknowledgements

We wish to thank the Tolson Memorial Museum for the photographs on pages 12 and 13; Mr Frank Atkinson for those on pages 14, 15, 16 and 17; and Mrs B Wordsworth, Stanleys Crumpets for those on pages 46 and 47.

Woman baking havercake, possibly in the Colne Valley, from Walker's *Costume of Yorkshire* (1814). A havercake steams on the bakestone situated on the left of the fireplace. The farmer's wife holds a backboard on which is a pool of batter. The bowl near the boy holds the batter and ladle. Several cakes are drying on a creel and on the upturned chair.

The Thirty-Third Regiment recruited during the American War in the neighbourhood of Halifax. The recruiting sergeant always preceded the party with a oatcake held on his sword, so that they were called the Havercake Lads. (*Costume of Yorkshire*)

James Mills shaping bakestones with a length of scythe blade at the quarry, whilst finished bakestones are hardening off in the water.

Arthur Schofield and James Mills making bakestones for baking oatcakes at the Bakestone Quarry near Delph. The bakestones have been quarried and dressed, and are baking round a fire in the hut. (1910)

The Oldroyd Brothers, commercial oatcake bakers, mixing the batter at their bakery at High Burton near Huddersfield. (1933)

Alfred Oldroyd putting the batter for one oatcake on the tram at High Burton.
The Oldroyds kept their recipe secret.

Mr J Wells in his Skipton bakehouse sprinkling the riddleboard with oatmeal before putting on a ladleful of batter. (1950s)

The pool of batter has been slid from the riddleboard on to the tram.

The pool of batter being thrown from the cloth on to the hotplate.

An oatcake is being loosened with a knife, and another oatcake dries on a cooler part of the hotplate.

Mr Leslie Feather, in his bakery at Haworth in 1965, begins to make oatcake. He dredges semolina on to a scored backboard. Note the crock containing the batter in the foreground.

Then he pours a ladleful of batter on to the board.

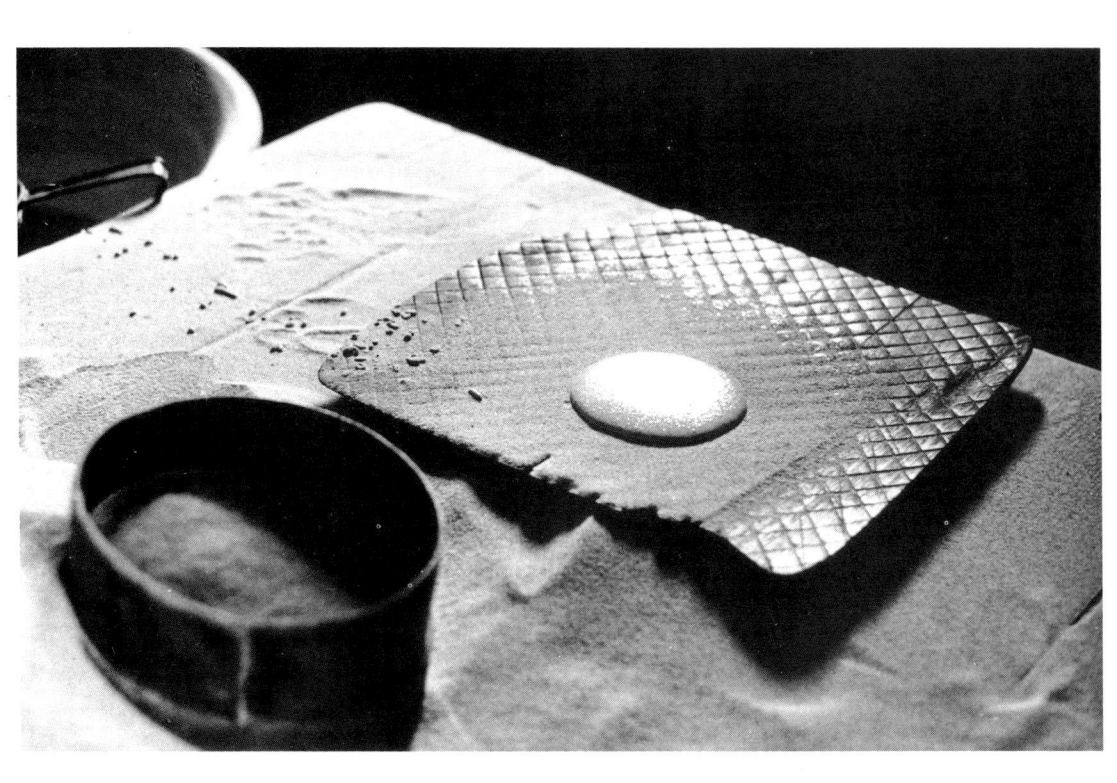

The round pool of batter on the backboard. It is a thick pouring consistency.

He takes the backboard and batter to the bakestone.

He transfers it on to the tram by drawing the board back quickly.
The front of the bakestone is shown here, as used by a public baker.

Note the two oatcakes in the foreground on the bakestone. The bakestone is now in the collection of the Cliffe Castle Museum at Keighley.

Cranking the lever to throw the oatcake from the tram on to the bakestone. This looks easy, but requires skill.

Loosening the cake with a bent knife in order to turn it over. The oatcake in the left corner of the photograph is drying on a cool part of the bakestone.

A baking of oatcake is placed on a wire tray. In 1965 it was sold for 3½d each.

The baker starts his rounds with a basket of oatcakes covered with a white cloth.

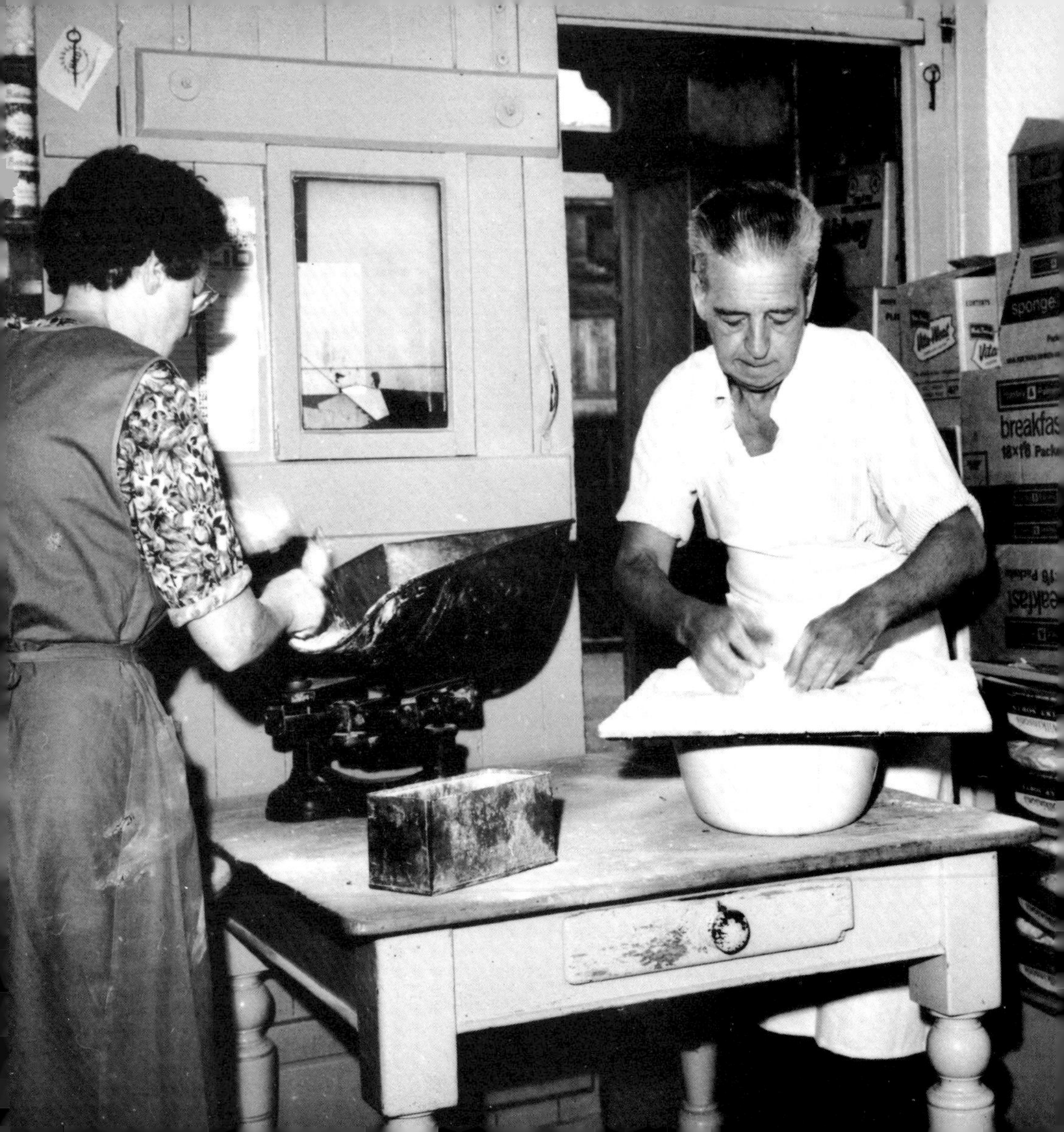
sponge

(Left) Mr and Mrs Feather making muffins. The Feathers worked as a partnership, as many did, and besides oatcakes they made muffins, crumpets and milk cakes.

(Right) Mr Feather making muffins.

Utensils for Baking Oatcake

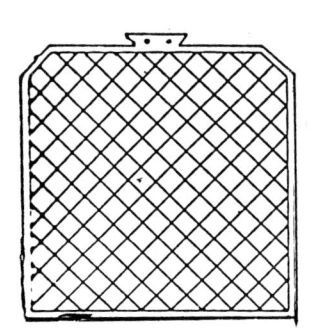

Riddleboard
or Riddling board
or Backboard

Hot Plate
Firebox
Door
grate

Bakestone

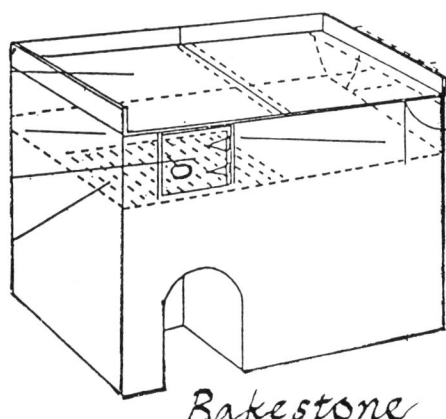

Scraper

Kneading tub

Cast iron backstone

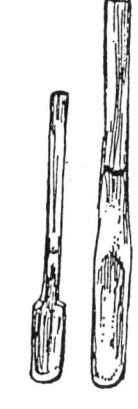

Thibles

ladle

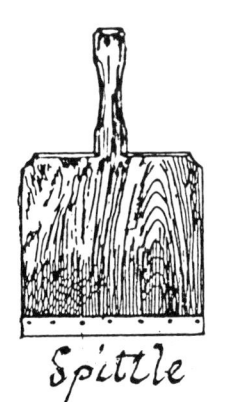

Spittle

Cake stools

A farmhouse kitchen with a bakestone alongside the range sharing the same flue. Both were removed in 1965. The bakestone is preserved at the Dales Countryside Museum, Hawes.

A bakestone alongside a fireplace in a back kitchen at Low Haycote, Dentdale. Both were disused and have been taken out.

A bakestone in an outhouse at Nether Hesleden, Littondale, and once used by Miss A Ingleby, who was noted for her oatcake. Moving to Kilnsey, and continuing to bake there, she had a large order book.

A bakestone in a house in Dentdale, with a large iron plate with shallow sides, typical of the Sedbergh/Howgill region. Here the paste was rolled out, rolled on to a turner (a long, thin rolling pin) and then unrolled on to the bakestone.

A stone bakestone at Knight Stainforth, Ribblesdale, with only the top stone left. Stone bakestones were rare.

A flake, pronounced *fleeak*, on which oatcakes were hung to dry in the kitchen of Archway Farm, Bolton Abbey. Usually they were left unpainted. 'Flake' was the name for this in the Dales, and 'creel' in the industrial West Riding.

Mrs E Carr at a farmhouse near Bentham stirs a mixture of oatmeal, water, yeast and carbonate of soda, ready for baking. (1966)

The bakestone is in an outhouse. She has poured on to it a ladleful of batter, and is drawing the scraper across it to make the oval shape.

She finishes thinning out with the scraper.

After loosening with a knife, the cake is turned.

The baked riddlebread is lifted with a baking spittle.

Then hung to dry on the flake in the kitchen.

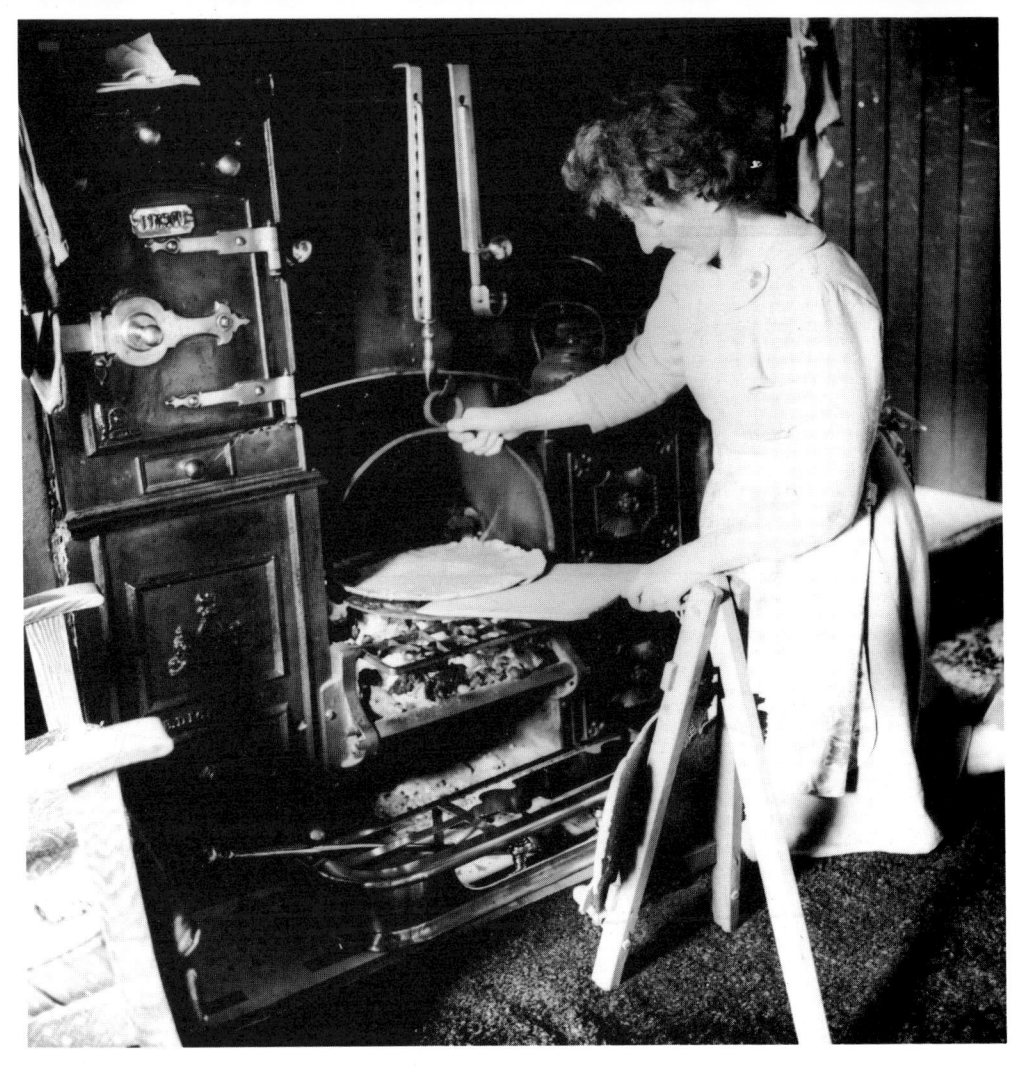

Baking the North Riding type of havercake at Keld, Swaledale.
Mrs J Alderson turns the cake.

The havercake is baking on the iron bakestone hung over the fire, and another cake dries on the cake stool.

Mrs Betty Wordsworth baking oatcake at Stanleys Crumpets bakery at Barnoldswick (1996). The bakery is equipped with a large cast-iron bakestone, on which several oatcakes may be baked at once. At one end is the tram for throwing the batter. She bakes eight to ten dozen an hour.

She turns an oatcake on the bakestone. Although the recipe has been modified by the addition of eggs, it is fair to say that the age-old tradition of baking thrown oatcake continues.